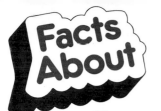

# Facts About

# Insects

## ELIZABETH COOPER

STECK-VAUGHN
LIBRARY
Austin, Texas

# How to Use this Book

This book tells you many things about insects. There is a Table of Contents on the next page. It shows you what each double page of the book is about. For example, pages 12 and 13 tell you about ''An Insect's Skin.''

On most of these pages there are some words that are printed in **bold** type. The bold type shows you that these words are in the glossary on pages 46 and 47. The glossary explains the meaning of some words that may be new to you.

At the very end of the book there is an index. The index tells you where to find certain words in the book. For example, you can use it to look up words like butterfly, pupa, caterpillar, and many other words to do with insects.

**Published in the United States in 1990 by Steck-Vaughn Co., Austin, Texas**, a subsidiary of National Education Corporation.

© Macmillan Children's Books 1988
Artwork © BLA Publishing Limited 1988

Material used in this book first appeared in Macmillan World Library: *The Insect World*. Published by Macmillan Children's Books

Designed by Julian Holland

Printed and bound in the United States
1 2 3 4 5 6 7 8 9 0 LB 94 93 92 91 90

**Library of Congress
Cataloging-in-Publication Data**

Cooper, Elizabeth.
  Insects.

  (Facts about)
  Summary: Introduces various types of insects, describing their skin, wings, eyes, feelers, life cycles, and environments; how they breathe and eat; and those that are pests and those that are helpful.
  1. Insects—Juvenile literature. [1. Insects] I. Title. II. Series: Facts about (Austin, Tex.)
QL467.2.C67  1990      595.7      89-21738
ISBN 0-8114-2506-1

# Contents

# The Busy World of Insects

Insects are everywhere on the Earth. Many are so small that we do not notice them. Some can live in places where other animals would not survive.

The hot springs in our picture are home for young **midges.** They are in Yellowstone Park in the northwestern United States.

**bees storing food**

**busy leaf-cutter ants**

Insects work hard. They use their feet and mouths for the special jobs they do. Insects build **nests.** They gather and store food. They feed their young. They must also keep safe from animals that like to eat them, especially the birds.

# What Is an Insect?

Insects belong to a big group of animals called **arthropods**. Our picture shows how they fit into this group.

An arthropod is an animal with **joints** in its body and legs. The joints help it to move easily.

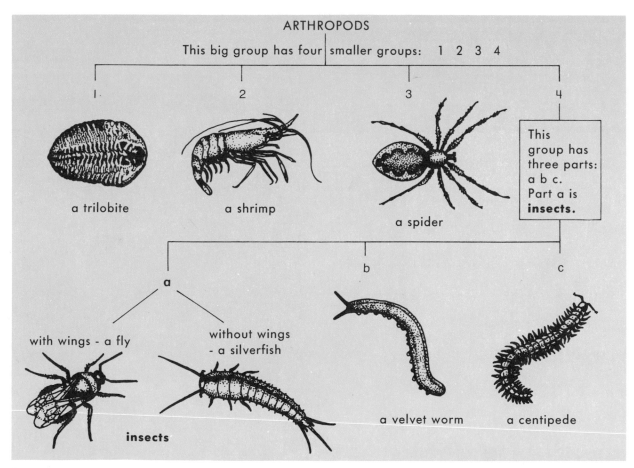

ARTHROPODS

This big group has four smaller groups: 1 2 3 4

1. a trilobite
2. a shrimp
3. a spider
4. This group has three parts: a b c. Part a is **insects**.

a — with wings - a fly / without wings - a silverfish

**insects**

b — a velvet worm

c — a centipede

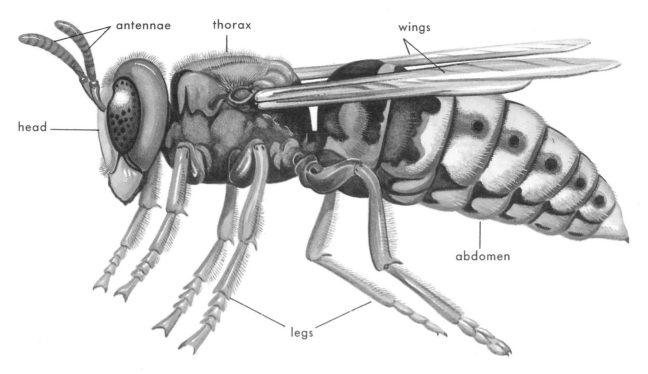

antennae    thorax    wings

head

abdomen

legs

## the parts of an insect

Our picture shows the main parts of an insect—the head, the **thorax**, and the abdomen.

Insects cannot keep warm in winter. They stay still like these ladybugs. In summer they warm up and move around.

## ladybugs in winter

# Insect Fossils

Huge insects used to fly in **swamps** like this 300 million years ago. We know this because people have found remains of insects in rocks. These remains are called **fossils.**

Some insect fossils have been found in a rock called **amber.**

Amber is the juice of pine trees that has become very hard. Insects used to feed on the sticky juice and get caught in it.

These fossils show us that insects must have been living on Earth long before the dinosaurs and a very long time before humans.

**an amber insect fossil**

**the insects' time on Earth**

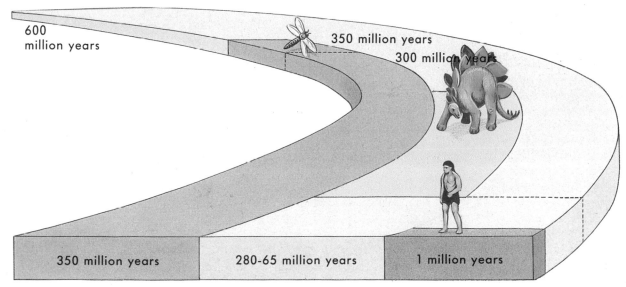

600 million years

350 million years

300 million years

350 million years

280-65 million years

1 million years

# Different Types of Insect

Most insects live on or near plants. Plants give them their food and their shelter. Sometimes insects even look like parts of plants!

There are thousands of different types of plants and insects. The box below tells you where some different kinds of insect live.

| Insects without wings | Where they live |
| --- | --- |
| Silverfish | in leaves and houses |

| Insects with wings (life cycle has three stages) | Where they live |
| --- | --- |
| Mayflies | larvae live in water, adults fly free |
| Dragon flies and damselflies | larvae live in water, adults fly free |
| Termites | in huge nests of soil |
| Grasshoppers and crickets | among plants |
| Leaf and stick insects | among plants |

| Insects with wings (life cycle has four stages) | Where they live |
| --- | --- |
| Lacewings and ant-lions | among plants and on the ground |
| Beetles | everywhere |
| Butterflies and moths | among plants |
| Bees, ants, and wasps | among plants and on the ground |

Sometimes insects need to change.

Some peppered moths changed their color to black because their favorite trees had turned black from factory smoke.

Mosquitoes have become used to certain **poisons.** Now these poisons do not harm them.

**two peppered moths—can you see the speckled one?**

**mosquitoes on a leaf**

# An Insect's Skin

## A dragonfly with its new skin

An insect has a hard skin called an **exoskeleton.**

It comes off each time the insect grows. Underneath there is a nice new skin.

Can you see the dragonfly's old skin?

## the middle part of an insect's body

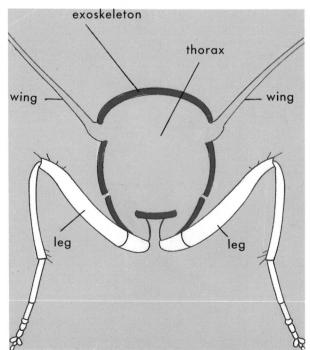

exoskeleton

thorax

wing

wing

leg

leg

**a bent caterpillar**

The body of an insect has many jobs to do.

The hard skin of an insect has hairs to help it feel, taste, and smell things.

The hairs take messages to the insect's brain.

Its body is made of bits or segments joined together so it can bend in all directions.

**hairs on a bee's leg**

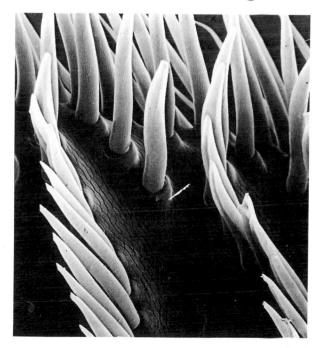

# Wings, Legs, and Feet

Wings help insects to fly away quickly from danger and to find their food. A wing is very strong because it is made of skin stretched over tubes called **veins**.

There are **muscles** in the insect's body that make the wing go up and down. When the wing goes up and down fast this makes the insect fly.

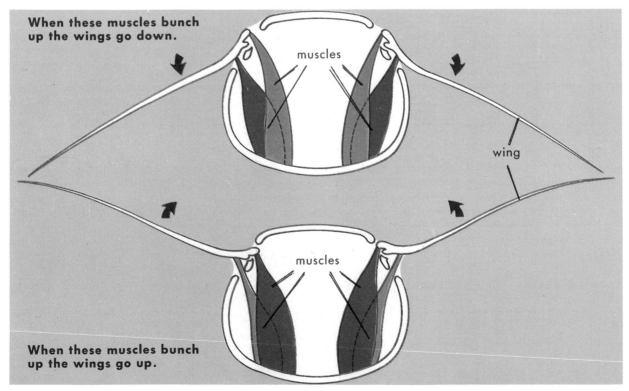

When these muscles bunch up the wings go down.

muscles

wing

muscles

When these muscles bunch up the wings go up.

**a yellow underwing moth**

An insect needs its legs and feet, too.

It may use them for running or for swimming or for jumping.

A pond skater uses its long thin legs to walk on water.

**a pond skater on water**

# Eyes and Feelers

Insects' eyes are different from ours.

Most young insects, called **larvae,** have several small eyes called simple eyes.

They cannot see shapes but they can tell night from day.

**a compound eye**

Most adult insects have two large eyes. These are called compound eyes.

They stick out from the insect's head so that it can see above, behind, and below.

**an insect can see all around**

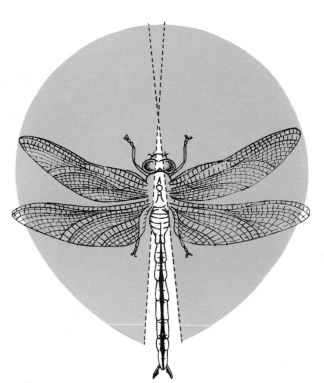

An insect feels, tastes, and smells with the hairs on its body. Stiff hairs called bristles tell the insect where it is safe to go.

Instead of noses, insects have **antennae** with hairs for smelling. The antennae of this luna moth look rather like green feathers.

# How Insects Breathe and Eat

An insect does not have **lungs** like larger animals.

It has very small holes called **spiracles** on the sides of its body.

Air passes through the holes and along tubes inside the insect.

**a spiracle blown up 200 times**

**insects have holes for breathing**

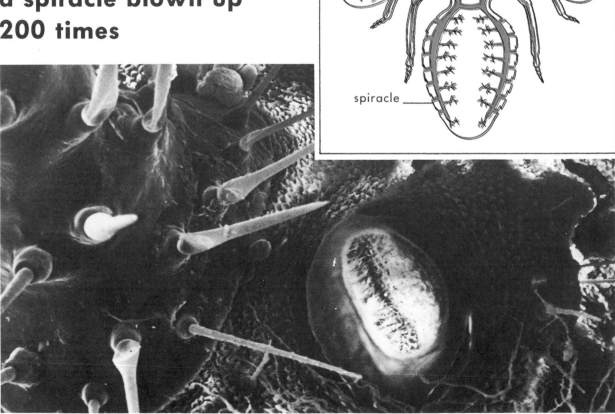

spiracle

The insect uses **oxygen** from the air to turn its food into energy.

It has a mouth to eat with. This tiger beetle has very strong jaws called **mandibles.** They have hard pointed tips for cutting food. Most insects eat plants or wood but some eat **dung,** hair, skin, or blood.

# The Life Cycle of an Insect

The way an insect changes and grows from an egg to an adult is called its life cycle. It can have three or four stages.

The young insect that comes out of the egg is called a **larva.** The grasshopper larva is called a nymph. It grows fast into an adult.

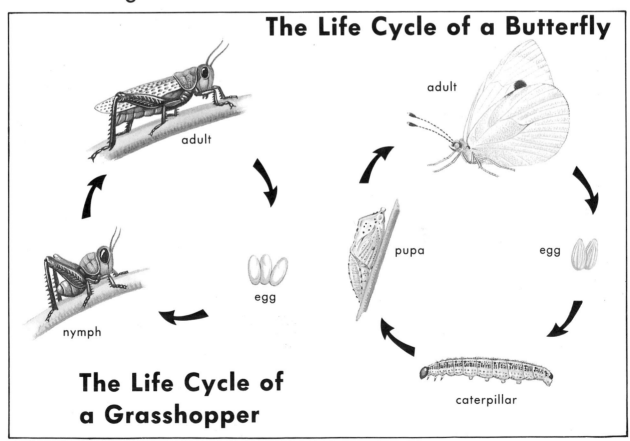

The Life Cycle of a Butterfly

adult

pupa

egg

caterpillar

adult

nymph

egg

The Life Cycle of a Grasshopper

A larva grows inside the insect egg. The butterfly larva is a caterpillar.

The caterpillar changes into a **pupa.** This is the resting stage for the insect to grow.

When the pupa opens, the adult insect, a butterfly, comes out.

**butterfly eggs**

**honeybee pupae**

# Insects Everywhere

Insects live in some surprising places.

The ant lion **larva** lives in sandy soil. It makes clever traps for ants.

The dune cricket lives in the desert. It has special feet to walk on the sand.

**a dune cricket**

**ant lion larva**

Some insects can lay hundreds of eggs at one time. If all of the eggs grew into adults there would be too many insects in the world.

Many insects are eaten by the birds. If many insects grow into adults they may move in large groups and eat a lot of food. This is called a plague of insects.

Sometimes locusts eat all the leaves off the farmers' crops.

# Making a Nest

Insects build their own **nests** or homes. Many make their own building materials.
These weaver ants use the **larvae** to make sticky silk thread for gluing leaves together. You can see a weaver ant holding a larva in the middle of the picture.

**tunnels and chambers inside an ants' nest**

Many ants build a nest like a mound above ground.

Inside there are tunnels and spaces called chambers. In one chamber the **queen ant** lays eggs.

The **worker ants** take the eggs to other chambers where they hatch into larvae.

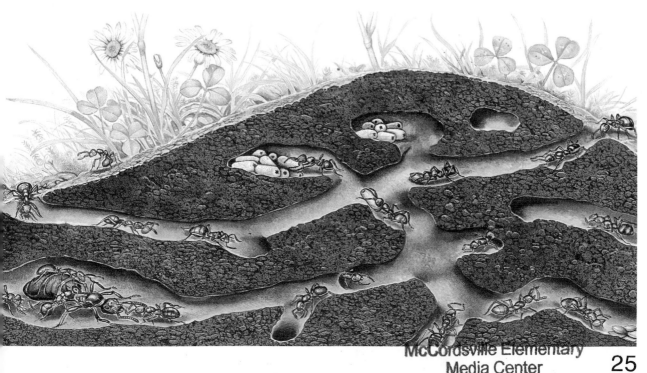

# Bees and Wasps

These honeybees are inside a **hive.** They are standing on nest **cells.** The **worker bees** make the cells from **wax.**

The **queen bee** has a red dot on her. She is laying an egg in each nest cell. The eggs will hatch into **larvae.** The larvae are fed by the worker bees.

When the queen bee leaves the **nest** the workers go with her.

They go in a **swarm.** This swarm is resting on its way to a new nest.

Wasps build their nests from a kind of paper that they make by chewing wood into **pulp**.

**a swarm of bees**

**a wasps' nest**

# Butterflies and Moths

Look at the butterfly and the moth. Can you see how they are different?

**a butterfly rests with wings closed**

**a moth rests with wings open**

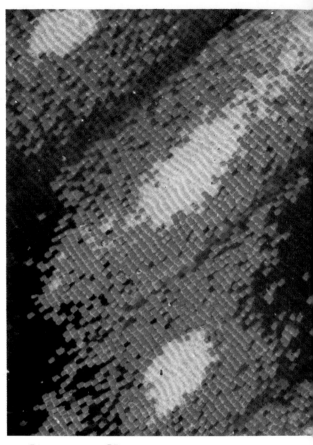

**a butterfly wing**

Butterflies fly during the day. Moths usually fly at night.

Their wings are covered in thousands of tiny **scales** that make up patterns.

The patterns help them to hide from their enemies.

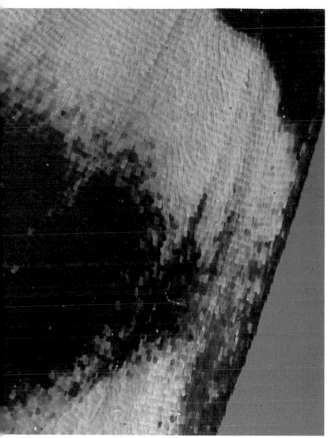

Some butterflies are copycats and are called mimics.

They have the same patterns as poisonous butterflies, but they are not really poisonous at all.

**a monarch butterfly caterpillar**

Sometimes the patterns scare enemies away.

Some are like eyes that frighten the birds. Other patterns are a warning to birds.

The bright stripes of the caterpillar in the picture warn the birds that it is poisonous.

# Jumping Insects

Crickets, grasshoppers, and locusts are all very good at jumping.

Grasshoppers make their sounds by rubbing their legs over a **vein** on the front wing.

Crickets rub the thick vein of one wing, called a file, over a pump on the other wing.

**a grasshopper on a flower**

## Insects Making Sounds

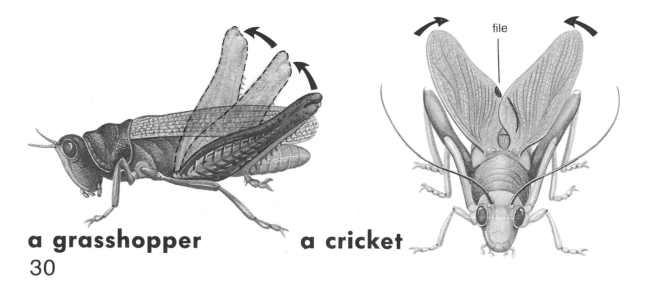

file

**a grasshopper**

**a cricket**

Locusts are big grasshoppers. They live in warm parts of the world. If there is plenty of food, many locusts grow into adults. They eat every plant in their way.

The man in the picture is walking through a **swarm** of these noisy insects. There can be millions of them in one swarm.

**Flies**

There are many insects that we call flies, but a true fly only has one pair of wings.

All true flies have mouths that suck. Some have mouths like needles for feeding on blood. This is how the mosquito carries **disease.**

The fly here is a blowfly. Its eggs hatch into **larvae** called **maggots.**

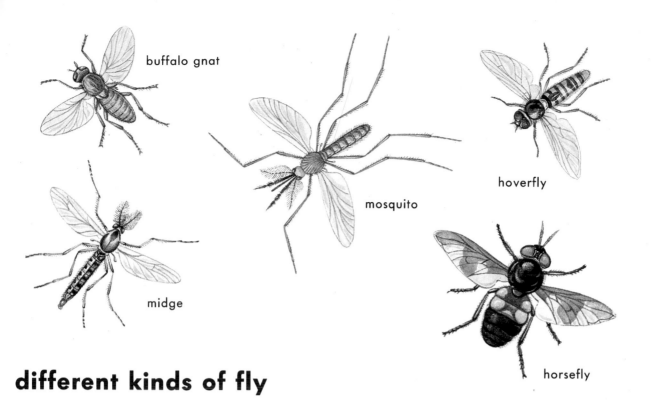

buffalo gnat

mosquito

hoverfly

midge

horsefly

## different kinds of fly

Many flies bite. You can see some of them in the picture.

The names of flies can often tell you something about them. A hoverfly can hover and a horsefly is large and bites horses and humans.

## a horsefly's large eyes

# Bugs and Beetles

Bugs and beetles are not the same. Bugs have mouths like needles and beetles have biting mouths.

Many bugs such as greenflies feed on the juices of plants or trees. A few bugs feed on blood from animals and humans.

Some bugs feed on other insects. The assassin bug in the picture has caught a bee.

## two blister beetles on a flower

Most beetles eat plants but the tiger beetle is fierce and eats other insects.

Leave blister beetles alone if you see any. They can make your skin come out in nasty blisters.

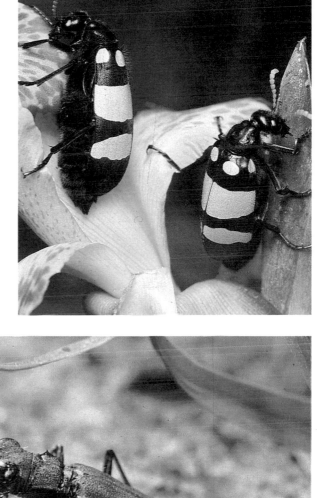

## a tiger beetle eating a larva

# Pond Insects

A pond is a home for many insects. The water contains small animals and plants that insects like to eat. Most of the insects in the water are **larvae.** The adults fly above the surface.

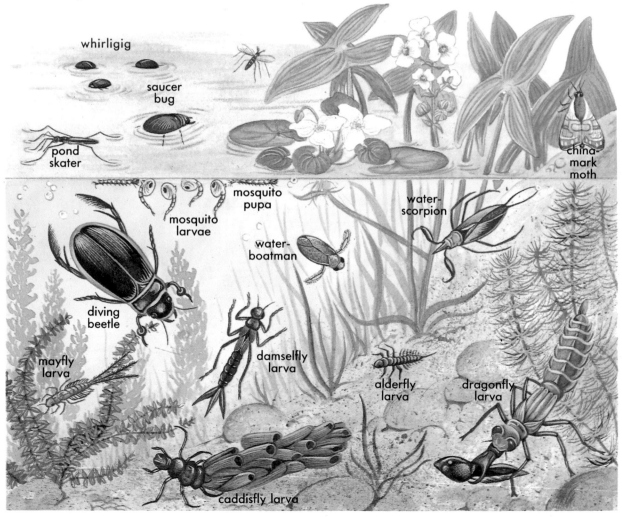

whirligig

saucer bug

pond skater

china-mark moth

mosquito pupa

mosquito larvae

water-scorpion

water-boatman

diving beetle

mayfly larva

damselfly larva

alderfly larva

dragonfly larva

caddisfly larva

**an adult dragonfly**

Can you see the dragonfly larva in the pond picture? It is catching a tadpole to eat.

When the larva is fully grown it will leave the water and turn into a beautiful dragonfly.

Some water insects dive and swim very fast to catch other small animals.

# Shapes and Colors

Insects try hard not to be eaten. Many have special shapes, colors, or patterns. They match the plants or ground around them so they cannot be seen easily. This is called **camouflage.**

Stick and leaf insects are camouflaged to look just like sticks and leaves.

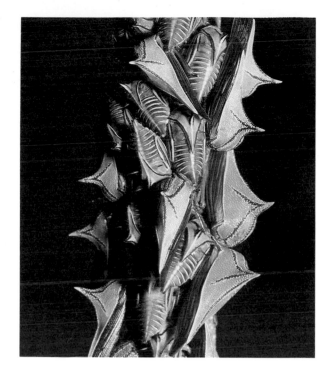

**treehoppers**

Other insects with a clever disguise are the treehoppers. They look just like sharp thorns, to trick the birds.

Sometimes male and female insects look very different. The male vaporer moth has big attractive wings.

The female has no wings at all. She spends her life laying eggs.

**vaporer moths**

female

male

# Insects in Our Homes

Our houses make nice safe homes for many insects.

Insect **pests** like the silverfish have places to hide and plenty of food to eat.

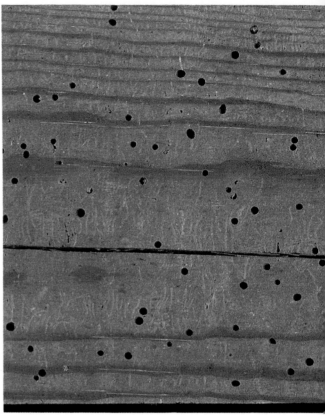

**a silverfish eating breadcrumbs**

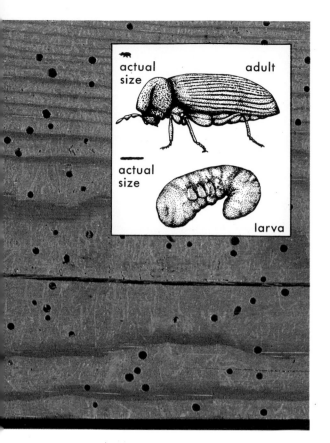

**a woodworm and the holes it makes**

Many insects that live in our homes came by ship from other places.

The woodworm or furniture beetle is an insect that once lived in dead trees. Now it eats holes in our furniture.

At night some insects come out of hiding.

The cockroach comes out to feed on bad food. It can pass on **germs** to fresh food.

It likes the dark. It runs away if a light is put on.

**cockroaches feeding**

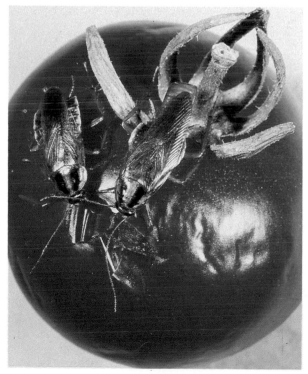

## Insect Pests

Some insects like to eat our crops.

White cabbage caterpillars eat our cabbages.

The Colorado potato beetle eats potatoes.

**cabbage white caterpillars**

Colorado beetles have eaten these potatoes

The fly in our picture is called a tsetse fly. It is feeding on human blood. Tsetse flies in Africa carry a disease called **sleeping sickness.**

Insect **pests** are a problem for us. People have made some special **poisons** that can kill the insects.

They are not very safe to use and they do not always work.

A safer way of getting rid of them is to get other insects to eat them.

# Our Insect Friends

Some insects are our friends. This
**hive** of honeybees is in an orchard.
The bees help the trees to make fruit.

44

Bees and other insects go to flowers to drink their **nectar.**

They pick up **pollen** on their feet and carry it to other flowers.

The pollen makes the flowers grow fruit or seeds.

Bees make **honey** and **wax** that we can use.

**a silkworm's cocoon**

Silkworms give us beautiful silk from their **cocoons.**

Some caterpillars in Australia help people by eating a weed called the prickly pear cactus.

**caterpillars on a prickly pear cactus**

45

# Glossary

**abdomen** the back part or tail of an insect.

**amber** the juice that came from pine trees millions of years ago and became very hard.

**antenna** a feeler on an insect's head. Each insect has two antennae that help it to smell.

**arthropod** an animal that has joints in its body and legs. It also has a hard outside skin. All insects are arthropods.

**camouflage** a special shape, color, or pattern that an insect has to match its surroundings. An insect with camouflage can hide from its enemies.

**cell** one small part of a bees' nest. There are hundreds of cells in a bees' nest. The bees make them from wax.

**cocoon** the case in which an insect grows.

**disease** an illness of a living animal or plant. Some insects can pass a disease from one animal or human to another.

**dung** droppings from animals.

**exoskeleton** the hard skin of an insect.

**fossil** the remains of an animal or a plant, usually found in rock.

**germ** a tiny animal that causes disease.

**hive** a house for bees to live in. Bees make honey in the hive.

**honey** a sweet sticky liquid that bees make from the nectar of flowers. The bees store honey in their nest.

**joint** the place where two parts of a body are joined. An insect has joints between the parts of its body and legs.

**larva** the second stage of an insect. The larva hatches out of an egg.

**lung** one of two parts of the body that an animal or human uses to breathe.

**maggot** the larva of a fly. It has no legs and moves by wriggling.

**mandible** an insect's strong biting jaw.

**midge** a tiny fly with two wings.

**muscle** a part of the body of an animal or human that makes another part move.

**nectar** the sweet liquid in flowers. Bees and other insects feed on nectar.

**nest** a home that some insects make for themselves.

**oxygen** a part of the air that animals need in order to breathe.

**pest** an animal that is a nuisance to humans. Some pests eat the food we grow or the things in our homes.

**poison** a harmful liquid or powder that can kill plants or animals.

**pollen** a kind of powder in the center of flowers.

**pulp** a soft mixture of chewed wood or plants and water.

**pupa** a resting stage in an insect's life cycle. Usually the insect is in a cocoon during this time.

**queen ant** a large female ant that lays eggs.

**scale** one of the many tiny parts that cover the wing of a butterfly or moth.

**sleeping sickness** a serious disease that is passed on from cattle to humans by the tsetse fly in Africa.

**spiracle** a vent or opening that lets air into an insect's body.

**swamp** an area of wet muddy land sometimes covered in shallow water.

**swarm** a large number of insects all moving together on their way to find a new nest.

**thorax** the middle part of an insect. The legs and the wings are joined to the thorax so the thorax is important for movement.

**vein** one of the many tubes in an insect's wing. The veins make the wing strong.

**wax** a substance made by bees and used by them to make the walls of their nest cells.

**worker ant** a female ant that does many jobs. It looks after the eggs and the larvae.

**worker bee** one of the many female bees that do all the work inside and outside the hive.

# Index

**Acknowledgments**
The Publishers wish to thank Rentokil and Shell for their invaluable assistance in the preparation of this book.
**Photographic credits** *(t=top b=bottom l=left r=right)* 4 ZEFA; 5t Stephen Dalton/NHPA; 5b, 7 Aquila; 9 Reproduced by permission of the Director, British Geological Survey (NERC); 11t Stephen Dalton/NHPA; 11b, 12 Aquila; 13t A Shell photograph; 13b Biophoto Associates/NHPA; 15t, 15b Stephen Dalton/NHPA; 16 Biophoto Associates/NHPA; 17 Anthony Bannister/NHPA; 18 Biophoto Associates/NHPA; 19 Keith Porter; 21t A Shell photograph; 21b Stephen Dalton/NHPA; 22 Anthony Bannister/NHPA; 23 a Shell photograph; 24 Ivan Polunin/NHPA; 25 Anthony Bannister/NHPA; 26, 27t Stephen Dalton/NHPA; 27b, 28/29 Aquila; 29b James Carmichael/NHPA; 30 Anthony Bannister/NHPA; 31 ZEFA; 32 Keith Porter; 33 G.J. Cambridge/NHPA; 31 ZEFA; 32 Keith Porter; 33 G.J. Cambridge/NHPA; 34 35t Anthony Bannister/NHPA; 35b Stephen Dalton/NHPA; 37 Anthony Bannister/NHPA; 35b Stephen Dalton/NHPA; 37 Anthony Bannister/NHPA; 38 Ivan Polunin/NHPA; 39 Aquila; 40b Stephen Dalton/NHPA; 40/41, 41b Rentokil; 42t Aquila; 42b A Shell photograph; 43 Anthony Bannister/NHPA; 44 Aquila; 45t Stephen Dalton/NHPA; 45b NHPA; cover and title page Stephen Dalton/NHPA